India-led Global Governance in the Indo-Pacific: Basis & Approaches, GLA-TR-003

Abhivardhan
President & Managing Trustee, Global Law Assembly

Poulomi Chatterjee
Contributing Researcher, Global Law Assembly

India-led Global Governance in the Indo-Pacific: Basis & Approaches, GLA-TR-003

Year: 2022
Date of Publication: February 15, 2022

ISBN (online): 978-81-954752-6-1

ISBN (paperback): 9798417065002

Authors: Abhivardhan & Poulomi Chatterjee

Printed and distributed online by Global Law Assembly in the Republic of India.

India-led Global Governance in the Indo-Pacific: Basis & Approaches, GLA-TR-003, First Edition 2022.

Price (Online): 200 INR

Price (Paperback). 10 USD (Amazon.com)

Global Law Assembly,
8/12, Patrika Marg, Civil Lines, Prayagraj,
Uttar Pradesh, India - 211001

The authorship of the book is retained with the authors of the technical report, while the ownership is retained by the publishing organization.

To cite, please follow the format for the list of references as follows:

2022. India-led Global Governance in the Indo-Pacific: Basis & Approaches, GLA-TR-003, *Prayagraj: Global Law Assembly, 2022.*

You can also cite the book through cite this forme.com (recommended) For Online Correspondence purposes, please mail us at executive[at]globallawassembly.org

For correspondence purposes, please contact at:
8/12, Patrika Marg,
Civil Lines, Prayagraj,
Uttar Pradesh, India - 211001

Preface

The Indo-Pacific Construct has various points of origin and it holds a special importance as a geopolitical construct for India. In this technical report, thus, the focus has been to propose to develop a multi-comprehensive approach (or at least a set of such approaches with some common & uncommon features, which is by all means, **Indo-centric (as proposed in this report)** (India-led, India-oriented) and reasonable. The report is not limited to the domain of international affairs, and thus, analyses the conceptual importance and relevance of the framework of the Indo-Pacific for practical reasons stated. We therefore look at various visionary considerations that are proposed, and even committed to by various countries, in the proposed geopolitical region. The following sub-portions discuss the most common and significant issues related to the conception of the Indo-Pacific in a distinctive manner.

The Indo-Pacific as a construct inspires the authors, and it would be a pleasure to contribute towards meaningful policy ideas and solutions to make Indo-Pacific more India-centric and sustainable. The authors provide special greetings to Mr Manohar Samal, Akash Manwani, Kartikey Misra, Dr Vignesh Ram, COVINTS and even Pratejas Tomar, Chief Executive Advisor, Global Law Assembly for their moral support.

Office of the Research Directorate
Global Law Assembly

Table of Contents

1 The Normative Indo-Pacific Construct: Common Issues and Degrees of Consensuses

1.1. What Constitutes ASEAN-centrality?

Though the meaning of ASEAN and the principle of ASEAN Centrality has mysteriously emerged between the lines, it is important to understand the most prominent vocabulary of Southeast Asia to maintain a cooperative and collaborative multipolar world. Thus, in the instant section, the meaning of ASEAN, ASEAN-centrality, and its nuances are described to elaborate the proposal of an Indo-centric Approach to Global Governance. It is believed that the association of ASEAN, which is an amalgamation of Southeast Asian Nations, took its form on 8th August 1967 in Thailand. It was called a legitimate association through the ASEAN Declaration (also often known as the Bangkok Declaration) which was signed by the five founding members of ASEAN, i.e., Indonesia, Malaysia, Singapore, Philippines, and Thailand. To constitute the present-day ASEAN with a total of ten member states, Brunei Darussalam joined the association on 7th January 1984, Vietnam on 28th July, 1995, Laos and Myanmar on 23rd July 1997, and Cambodia on 30th April 1999.

Across the years of American unipolarity, ASEAN has had a role in creating major regional mechanisms like that of the ASEAN Regional Forum (ARF) and the East Asia Summit (EAS) which confers the ability of ASEAN to act as another key player in the emerging multipolar world. Through platforms like the ASEAN Regional Forum (ARF) and the East Asia Summit (EAS), the association can collate and manage their interactions in the Southeast Asian region. Through the ASEAN centric approach, the association aims to widen the concept of ASEAN-centrality, which essentially translates into better regional security and economic processes in the region of Southeast Asia (Hyome, 2020). However, despite the emergence of ASEAN Centrality, its meaning remains unclear (Acharya, 2017 pp. 273-279). Since the term has become a part of the prominent vocabulary of the international relations in context of Southeast Asia, especially Asia as a continent in general, it is important to understand the same.

Initially, 'ASEAN Centrality' was referred to as the prime driving force of the wider East Asian and Asia-Pacific regionalism, as has been established in the ASEAN Charter and the initial summits of the ASEAN and related bodies, i.e., according to the documents of the 2nd East Asia Summit (EAS), the 10th Asia Plus Three (APT) Summit, and the 12th ASEAN Summit, all of which were held in 2007. The vagueness of the above documents, however, has led to the emergence of myths in association with the term of ASEAN individually and ASEAN Centrality. Through the above-mentioned documents, ASEAN is essentially an actor which promotes its body as the architect for explicitly forming the nucleus of the regional processes and institutional designs involved in the construct of Asia-Pacific. However, it is often commonly misunderstood about the fact that the ASEAN is not primarily only involved in the Southeast Asian Region, but rather acts as another player in the larger dynamics of regionalism not only specific to the Asia-Pacific, but even beyond (Kraft, 2011 p. 63).

Hence, viewed at large, the emergence of ASEAN as an association seems to be more in relation to dealing with the dynamics of the emerging multipolar order and the great power relationships it comes with, rather than simply promoting the identity of ASEAN as Southeast Asia and its unity. In totality, the idea of ASEAN Centrality refers to the necessity of the core interests of Asia-Pacific regional institutions to remain as its nucleus.

Furthermore, in this context, it is also established through the principle of ASEAN Centrality that ASEAN acts as a blueprint or a model for other subregional institutions existing in the Asia-Pacific region and beyond. It has been witnessed in history, for ASEAN's initial years to be followed keenly by the western power, especially in terms of the British documents of that period (Acharya, 2014). This signifies that the initial construct of ASEAN could not have imagined the association of ASEAN to be able to achieve a sense of 'centrality' in the wider Asia-Pacific region. Through the influence of ASEAN, not only did the association fulfill its aims in the Asia-Pacific region, but also beyond in the Indian Ocean.

Thus, this brings us to the question whether in terms of geography, Europe and other landlocked countries near the Indian Ocean can also be considered a part of the Indo-Pacific which stands as a more modern term than Asia-Pacific. To understand the relevance of landlocked countries in the regional construct, however, it is also important to understand how the Indo-Pacific emerged and how it translates in terms of ASEAN Centrality. In context of this, the External Affairs Minister of India, Dr S Jaishankar claims that India's sole relationship with the ASEAN is one of the key pillars of achieving its own share of **sturdy foreign policy**, as well as a foundation for its Act East Policy. In this sense, it is essential to note that India's Act East Policy is yet another diplomatic approach for promoting economic, strategic, as well as cultural relations in the Asia-Pacific region, which is also in line with the core interests of ASEAN, it being a model for other subregional institutions existing in the Asia-Pacific region, such as India's Act East Policy in the instant context.

To convey its interests upon the ASEAN, India had approached the United Nations Security Council (UNSC) recently in April 2021, to admit that the vision of Indo-Pacific which translates smoothly as a free, open, and inclusive region is knitted in the notion of ASEAN Centrality since the beginning (Hyome, 2020). Thus, according to the humble and ambitious minds of India, a coordinated and concentrated action between the ASEAN and the Indo-Pacific would assist the region in combating contemporary security and regional complexes. Furthermore, the recognition of the Indo-Pacific replacing the Asia-Pacific simply means that the region is trying to strategically compete with foreign influences like that of China.

The Quadrilateral Security Dialogue, or more commonly referred to as the QUAD which has recently took its form, has acquired its main mission to expand the cooperation in the Indo-Pacific region by essentially working towards a free and open Indo-Pacific, free from Chinese and western efforts of growing influence in the region. Interestingly, the notion of ASEAN Centrality in fact gained larger momentum with China's growing influence and predominance across the region, which forced the association to keep the area's security and inclusiveness in mind, while partnering up with the QUAD and replacing Asia-Pacific from the Indo-Pacific (Hyome, 2020).

1.2. The Geography: Land and Sea

The intent behind the making of the Indo-Pacific was to cope up with the rising transnational threat, especially due to the emerging regional complexes slowly shifting America's unipolar order into a multipolar order, including threats of Chinese expansion and retainment of Russian legacy. It is also noteworthy to note in interest of the common heritage of mankind in the Indo-Pacific, is the strategic claims of China wanting to expand from its existing territory towards the South China Sea, to the East China Sea, and its rapid advance towards the Indian Ocean through selfish initiatives like the Belt and Road Initiative (BRI), all of which has challenged the Indo-Pacific region to come under an international rules-based system (Harris, 2020 pp. 1-5). Thus, amongst this, the Indo-Pacific has been constructed in order to defend the regional order of all those countries which constitutes the Indo-Pacific. For this, it is imperative for us to understand the core geographical parameters when it comes to constituting the Indo-Pacific.

In this sense, the Prime Minister of India, Shri Narendra Modi had declared on his keynote speech at Shangri-La Dialogue of 2018, that the geographical boundary of the Indo-Pacific **consists of the Indian Ocean as well as the**

Western Pacific. However, for the US, the Indo-Pacific region ends at the Indian coastline itself, for it in order to be able to maintain the US Indo-Pacific command (Siddiqui, 2019). Shri Narendra Modi, the Prime Minister of India, in his keynote speech of the Shangri-La Dialogue in 2018, highlighted the geographic essence of the Indo-Pacific, by stating that the same starts from Africa to America, which is able to cover both the Indian Ocean as well as the Western Pacific Oceans, which includes the territory of Japan. Moreover, when American fingers were raised towards China not being a part of the Indo-Pacific construct, for maintaining the policy of inclusiveness in ASEAN Centrality, India ensured that the Indo-Pacific is a construct for the whole region (Siddiqui, 2019).

The Indo-Pacific has become such a part of a geopolitical nomenclature, that it is being considered as the geographical and strategic construct in context of the foreign policy of Japan, US, Australia, India, and France, including the Southeast Asian states involved in the Association of Southeast Asian Nations (ASEAN), which has successfully replaced the terminology of 'Asia-Pacific' (Hemmings, 2018 p. 17). The two oceans involved in the region of the Indo-Pacific, namely the Indian Ocean and the Western Pacific Ocean, constitute of the whole region, which conveniently matches with the fact that the majority of the world's goods and energy supplies are transported via these two oceans. Thus, it is not surprising for the Indo-Pacific to be able to emerge as a major player in today's geopolitical arena (Heiduk, et al., 2020 p. 7).

As of today, the United States has defined the Indo-Pacific region in terms of geography as stretching from the Western Pacific Ocean, till the mid of the Indian Ocean, halting at the coastline of India. According to the American vision of a Free and Open Indo Pacific (FOIP), the Indo-Pacific covers the US overseas territories in the Western Pacific Ocean, consisting of Guam and American Samoa, and takes all other nations and islands that border these two oceans under its wing (US Department of State, 2019).

For India, however, the Indo-Pacific translates geographically into involving a part of the Indian Ocean, covering the member states involved in the Quadrilateral Security Dialogue (QUAD) and the countries in relation to the Association of Southeast Asian Nations (ASEAN).

Furthermore, for Australia, the Indo-Pacific geographically constitutes of the entirety of the Indian Ocean, covering Madagascar, Mauritius, New Zealand, and other small islands in the territory, almost similar to the ideology of India, but wider in its concept (Heiduk, et al., 2020; Australian Government, 2017).

For Japan, all the three ideologies are grouped together to promote the principle of inclusiveness towards all. Thus, for Japan, the Indo-Pacific region is construed to include the entire area spanning from the east coast of Africa to the American Pacific coast (Heiduk, et al., 2020). This is because, as Japan has gained confidence after the momentum of QUAD and the Indo-Pacific, it expects the Indo-Pacific to be the next in line towards a multipolar order.

For this reason, it is also interestingly noted that the Association of Southeast Asian Nations (ASEAN), the Indo-Pacific has not been defined in the formal documents of the association (Heiduk, et al., 2020).

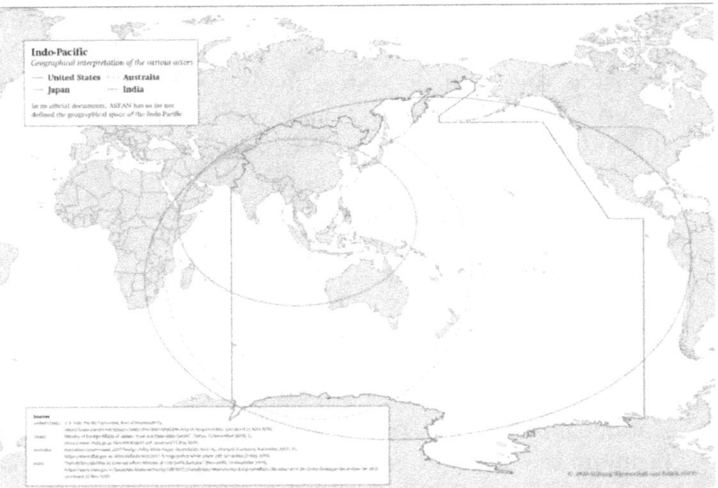

Figure 1: Geographical Interpretation of the Indo-Pacific According to Various States (Heiduk, et al., 2020)

On November 2017, former President Donald Trump of the US presented his strategic idea of the Free and Open Indo Pacific (FOIP) at the Asia-Pacific Economic Cooperation (APEC) summit in Hanoi, after the former President Barack Obama had outlined the Indian Ocean and the Western Pacific Ocean to form its own ideology of the Indo-Pacific region (US Mission to ASEAN, 2017). Furthermore, former President Barack Obama also highlighted American plans for creating an Indo-Pacific Economic Corridor (IPEC) in addition to the political and military "pivot to Asia" (Heiduk, et al., 2020) (Scott, 2018 pp. 19-43).

Quite recently, the European Union has agreed to formulate its own strategy for the Indo-Pacific as well, once it realised that it is economically dependent on the network stretching from the Indian Ocean to the Western Pacific Ocean. Furthermore, the European Union High Representative, Mr. Josep Borrell also claimed that the Indo-Pacific has achieved enough power to be able to represent the world as its economic and strategic centre of gravity (Basu, et al., 2021; EEAS, 2021b). Thus, if the stability of the Indo-Pacific is in threat due to intense geopolitical competition, the interests of the European Union are also hindered, explained Mr.

Borrell (Morcos, 2021). This is majorly due to the fact that the European Union identifies itself as a supporter of the Indo-Pacific (EEAS, 2021a). However, despite Europe's deep involvement in the Indo-Pacific region since decades, the Indo-Pacific does not recognize its overall influence. Connecting the dots from this state, it is justifiable how Europe's activities in the Indo-Pacific are uncoordinated and disjointed, especially when it comes to capacity-building projects or maritime patrols (Morcos, 2021).

Unafraid of addressing this issue, the European Union has attempted time-specific strategies on connectivity issues and maritime security issues but was never completely successful in comprehensively being able to implement its policies. Moreover, the member states of the European Union have shown clear intent to establish an EU Strategy to the Indo-Pacific, ensuring a joint communication, which would then translate into terms of smooth trade agreements to connectivity investments to maritime security (Morcos, 2021). Referring to the European Union's 'Connecting Europe and Asia' strategy of 2018, the union provides a strong alternative to China's Belt and Road Initiative (BRI) to increase transparency, sustainability, and encourage local ownership and self-reliance (Morcos, 2021) (European Commission, 2018). Considering the threat of Chinese dominance over the region, the European Union's hand promising inclusivity translates into a smoother Indo-Pacific future (Heiduk, et al., 2020).
However, it is clear that the Indo-pacific has not taken into consideration the strategic interests of the European Union, since the intent of the Indo-Pacific is majorly said to be inclined towards maritime security most. In other words, the construct of Indo-Pacific considers India as its centre point, which leads us to the probable school of thought that all strategic planning of the Indo-Pacific is favourable largely for India. Thus, this leaves us in question as to whether the landlocked countries like Europe matter to the construct of the Indo-Pacific or not. Amongst the strategic construct of the Indo-Pacific, one thing can be denoted for sure; if the Indo-Pacific is construed in a manner which is favourable to major players in the geopolitical arena, it may be the next in

line to receive the crown in context of a multipolar order. In this context, it is also noteworthy to note that the geographical definition of the Indo-Pacific has been loosely construed as stretching from the Indian Ocean to the Western Pacific; an idea which may be developed further, keeping in mind the strategic interests of other geopolitical players (Basu, et al., 2021).

Asia-Pacific to Indo-Pacific: The Basis of an Indo-centric Approach

Quoting the words of Stanley Hoffmann, all nations across the globe believe themselves to be unique in their own way, however, only few can stand out and come under the spotlight. One such country is that of the United States, which has attempted its golden hand on foreign policies such that it has remained in a state of global hegemony for decades (Nye, 2019 pp. 63-80). The American led hegemony resulted in the emergence of efficient security alliances, multilateral institutions, as well as open economic policies, all of which are together translated into an American International Order, i.e., a Liberal International Order followed globally. In this manner, the country became the world's largest economy which left its influence till a long period of time, which is beginning to crack only recently in the 21st century. In the current age, especially after the emergence of the deadly COVID-19 pandemic, the arena of geopolitics has become more active wherein countries have started to realize their own potential of becoming self-sufficient. It is noteworthy to mention that China has posed a difficult stance towards the American global hegemony, simply because it has become a new force which had risen quietly but rapidly over the years. Nations across the globe realized that the liberal international based order is a threat to them gradually, as the United States went through the transformation of being a global hegemonic power to being an imperialist ideology (Smith, 2017 p. 232). Many foreign policy experts opined that China may take upon the dangling responsibility of the United States, marking an end of the American era, however, it is strongly believed by the west that the Chinese influence is not to overthrow the prevailing American order, but to simply benefit and influence itself within that order, such that the Chinese power continues to grow. However, in any case scenario, if the Chinese power continues to grow, or if any other power stronger than that of the United States emerges, the American liberal order is at a pressure point to change (Nye, 2018).

In this context, it is imperative to understand how the Chinese influence and rise of power came about in order to understand the transition from Asia-Pacific to Indo-Pacific. For almost the whole period led by the American global hegemon, i.e., approximately 70 years, the order in the Asia-Pacific region, which was also often referred to as the region of 'Pax Americana,' remained unchanged and unquestioned, under the dominance of the United States. However, after the first decade of the 21st century, China began to pick pace in its manufacturing industry and out took the United States by becoming the world's largest manufacturing superpower after the United States itself. In this light, China then began formulating strategies in favor of its own interests to retain its footprint on the geopolitical arena, such as by introducing the Belt and Road Initiative (BRI), i.e., initiatives that would assist the country in reshaping the international rules-based order according to Chinese proclamations (Heiduk, et al., 2020).

Amongst all this, however, the strategic interests of India were not taken, for which the country then established its own favorable path of the Indo-Pacific, which certain other major players of the geopolitical arena assumed to be beneficial in their own interests, because India has been gifted with natural borders and effective and efficient instincts. However, even after the emergence of the Indo-Pacific, India struggled to find an inward-looking strategy which could benefit itself the most, by partnering with other interested nations. Based on this, an Indo-centric approach must be carved out which can directly respond to the challenges posed by other key and major players in the geopolitical arena.

In this context, it is imperative for India to remain as the center of the Indo-Pacific strategy to allow the emergence of an equally strong and efficient force which can outperform the Chinese influence as well as the American dominance. Furthermore, it is interestingly observed that the Indian state is a natural influencer without having to step into the means of sponsorship, political imposition, or concrete efforts (Pulipaka, et al., 2021). For example, India and Vietnam share an ages old connection, possibly originating from the Cham civilization. Moreover, Indonesia's nomenclature is derived from the Greek words 'Indos' and 'Nesos,' which together form the magical phrase of 'Indian Islands.' Thus, from this, the Indian culture has not only inspired other cultures but is also a strong forefront that can be used through the Indo-Pacific strategy in order to bring about a fair, just, and apparently liberal based order.

1.3. Scope for the Development of International Law

In the arena of geopolitics, it is known to us that most countries are not rather concerned about the global good, but only take into their own self-interests, which translates into smooth trade-off situations. This means that countries would willingly help other countries if they are able to reap some benefit out of their investments, i.e., a trade-off. For example, the trade policy which translates into the most problematic part of the Free and Open Indo Pacific (FOIP) strategy simply emerges because it is guided by the principle of America First (Heiduk, et al., 2020). Thus, any and every initiative supporting innovative mechanisms are sure to be impacting the US businesses in a positive way. At the same time, the Indo-Pacific also benefits from the investments of the United States but has to endure the pickles of the biased principle of 'America First.' The implementation of the America First Principle has thus often originated conflicts between the group of nations stitched together in the Indo-Pacific, rather than bringing them closer to the American Trade Policy terms, taking into consideration both their considerations.

In context of Japan, the Indo-Pacific and the construct of the Free and Open Indo Pacific (FOIP) is considered to be an alternative to China's Belt and Road Initiative (BRI), considering that the Chinese Belt and Road Initiative (BRI) has been majorly responsible for setting the new international standards of development (Koga, 2020). Hence, Japan's involvement in the Indo-Pacific is simply aimed at ruling out Chinese influence. If taken on another stance, however, Japan has not cut off its ties with China due to its continued engagement with the country in relation to drafting the fifth symbolic official document after the 1972 Sino-Japanese diplomatic normalization which played a major role in highlighting the future visions of the Sino-Japanese relations (Koga, 2020 pp. 21-27). Thus, the path to future is still foggy, but it is clear that Japan may or may not join in on behalf of the Indo-Pacific, since its true interest lies in being in contact with a powerful source, which may be through the path of its ally, i.e., United States or the most powerful start-up, i.e., China.

For the Association of Southeast Asian Nations (ASEAN), the emphasis of ASEAN unity and centrality became more prominent in 2018, after which the ASEAN Chair issued the ASEAN Outlook on the Indo-Pacific (AOIP) statement in 2019 (Ministry of Foreign Affairs of Japan, 2018). The ASEAN Outlook on the Indo-Pacific (AOIP) statement focussed on the elements of inclusivity of regional architecture and regional cooperation over stances of rivalry, which can be matched with the ASEAN's priority of neutralizing rivalry in the region pertaining to Southeast Asia and other subregions of the Indo-Pacific. Thus, the stance of ASEAN is still not clear in regards to the Quadrilateral Security Dialogue (QUAD) and the Indo-Pacific, since an effective multilateralism cannot be traced through the vague dialogues proposed by the ASEAN Secretariat, since the same would be viewed as diplomatic marginalization (US Department of State, 2020).

Furthermore, it is noteworthy to also mention that the Association of Southeast Asian Nations (ASEAN) is of special importance to the Indo-Pacific due to the fact that Southeast Asia is considered to be the geographical centre of the region. According to Japan, without the involvement of the Association of Southeast Asian Nations (ASEAN), an international rules-based order for uniting the Western

Pacific and the Indian Ocean will not be possible (Koga, 2020). In this context, it is also imperative to note that India is considered a major factor in bringing a smooth multipolar world of Asia, but it must not be treated as a mere 'balancer' to defend the American interests, and instead be considered as a major player to the Indo-Pacific as well as the rest of the world, considering the Indian strategy of exerting itself as the shaper of global order (Basu, 2020 pp. 21-27).

To understand why there is a larger scope for the development of international laws, it is imperative for us to understand the stances of the current emerging powers in the geopolitical arena. In the Chinese context, the pursuit for achieving a narrative of power comes from its historical interpretation of the Century of Humiliation which took place in the First Opium War through the Sino-Japanese War (Basu, 2020). Thus, since the 19th Century of Humiliation, China built its stance against the west by seeking balance between the current asymmetric distribution of powers and benefits in the international community. Collective efforts from the Chinese Communist Party (CPP) are visibly apparent in context of the grand Belt and Road Initiative (BRI) aside from other solutions to major international issues, through which China has posed a difficult challenge to the American global power projection through its rising predominance.

In a similar manner, the views of India have been much in-line regarding the US-led liberal order, which is constituted as the foundation for the Indo-Pacific construct. It is interestingly observed that along with the rapidly rising dominance of China and its influence, India has had to face Chinese aggression alongside its common border with the country. Although India has been able to manage the encounters of Doklam, Chumar, and Depsang, the incident in relation to Galwan has left India on its tiptoes, ever since Beijing strategically lost India (Basu, 2020; Krishnan, 2020). Hence, after such encounters, India has had to consider the possible impact of Chinese predominance on the Indo-Pacific territory, which led to the formation of the construct of the Indo-Pacific.

In the western context, however, although the Trump administration pursued a gentler method of treating the country as compared to China, India is aware of the possibility of selfish self-interests and trade-off situations to take place, which gives rise to the strategic thinking of India and its strategy of engagement-with-all without having the need to choose between rival powers in the current geopolitical arena (Basu, 2020). This is majorly because India does not shy away from the fact that the United States has the power to conduct a grand bargain with China, which is why India demands a balance of interest amongst the international community, which has also been coined as the guiding principle of India's foreign policy (Basu, 2020). Through this, it can be observed that neither the construct of Indo-Pacific, nor India as a country can completely be able to trust the American soft power regime, mainly because it has witnessed the formation of conflict economies in a similar manner.

An individual country attains its soft power from three main sources, i.e., (1) its culture, i.e., the main factor that attracts the other nations, (2) its political values, i.e., through which individual countries form their reputation and humility (e.g., when a country is aware of the circumstances of another country and is ready to give and support them), and lastly, (3) its policies, i.e., which denotes how a country handles its own interests at home, in the international community, as well as in foreign policy (Nye, 2018). In this context, the American soft power regime has seen a steep decline in recent times, which is especially noticeable after the Bush Administration. In this matter however, several scholars would admit that the boom and decline of soft power does not play a role in determining the outlook of a country majorly due to the bitter fact that countries cooperate with each other purely out of self-interest to create situations of trade-offs. However, it must also be noted that the act of cooperation must also be affected by a certain degree of attraction or repulsion (Nye, 2018).

1.4. What Includes Resilience?

It has recently flashed in our minds in regards to why the majority of tags, labels, and stickers on a variety of goods proclaim the title, 'Made in China.' It is also strangely observed that the world economy has started criticizing what are the actual methods that are used by China for it to successfully become the World's Manufacturing Superpower, especially after the United Nations Statistics Division declared that China is responsible for 28.7 percent of the global manufacturing output in 2019. This number further signifies that the country is more than 10 percentage points ahead of the United States which in turn used to be the former largest manufacturing sector in the world, until China emerged as a manufacturing superpower in 2010 (United Nations Statistics Division, 2000).

Since the world economy encountered several climate disasters, natural mishaps, and unexplainable Acts of God, it is important for us as responsible citizens to ensure environmental safety first of all, while also adhering to the principles of Corporate Social Responsibility (CSR) before taking part in the buying, selling, and the manufacturing processes of goods which are prepared in questionable ways (Bachhawat, et al., 2020). Hence, a stronger and a more reliable source of Global Supply Chains is extremely important in order for the economy to move along in the path of development and sustainability. For this, however, the Chinese methods of becoming the world's manufacturing superpower is important to study. Furthermore, in this section, the promotion of the Indian country to become the next big superpower is explained and given a way to, which can prove to become the better and more reliable source of a Global Supply Chain than that of China.

Due to the presence of these reasonable factors, a number of nations across the globe have resorted to inward looking policy formulation which would ultimately benefit their own countries, instead of depending on the manufacturing superpower of China and its strong and efficient Global Supply Chain. This, however, has hindered the progress of Globalisation 5.0, which is said to be led by new-age science and technological innovations (Sharma, et al., 2021). In the earlier phases of globalisation, technology, energy, and trade were the engines which supported the process. However, in the instant state of affairs, Globalisation 5.0 can only be achieved if the states' behaviour is improved accordingly, and a benefitting strategy for all is approved upon. This points us towards the possibility of the Indo-Pacific leading the process of Globalisation 5.0 by being the centre of such strategy formulation.

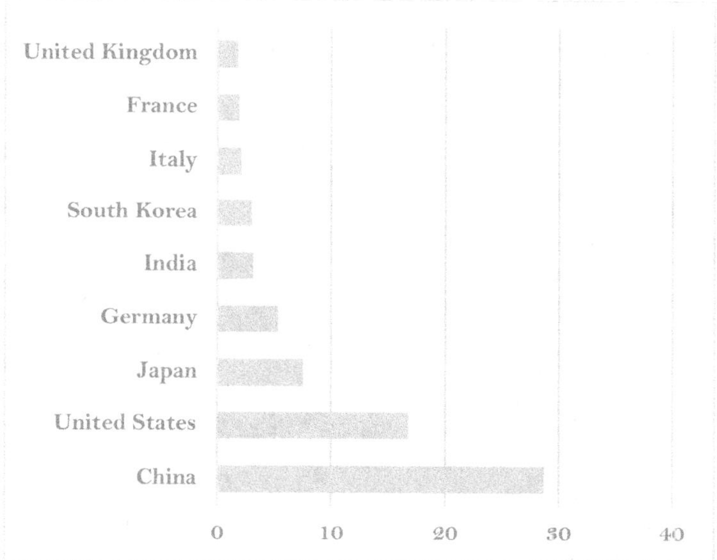

Figure 2: Global Manufacturing Output in 2019 (United Nations Statistics Division, 2000)

In a nutshell, it has been witnessed that the Chinese manufacturing industry operates on the basis of low taxes and duties, lack of regulatory compliance, and competitive currency practices (Bajpai, 2021). To further elaborate on this issue, it is observed that while the manufacturing industry belonging to the west mandatorily complies with appropriate health, safety, and environmental regulations, the manufacturing industry at China operates much more permissively. Furthermore, to bring about a lower price of its goods as compared to American competitors, China has often been accused of using artificial methods to decrease the value of its currency (Garton, et al., 2005; Tan, 2018).

In this context, on the other hand, to cope up with the dependence of the Indo-Pacific region on Chinese supply chains, Japan has proposed the Supply Chain Resilience Initiative (SCRI) along with India and Australia to increase flexibility of choices between a variety of supply chains (Kumar, 2020). It is also noteworthy to mention that the importance of the Supply Chain Resilience Initiative (SCRI) was discussed and affirmed upon in the 2+2 ministerial meeting which was held between India and Australia earlier this September (Ministry of External Affairs, Government of India, 2021a). Through this, we observe that the government of India has taken a mission on its bucket of transforming the country into a global hub of supply chains which is comparatively better and more ethical than that of China. It is clear that this initiative would not only allow India to benefit economically, but also deepen its relations with other trade countries. For this purpose, India has proposed to partner with its key trading partner Australia in order to allow a seamless integration into the Global Value Chains (GVCs), with the key goal in mind to strengthen international supply chains (Press Information Bureau, Government of India, 2021).

According to Minister Shri Piyush Goyal, the Australia-India Business Champions Group will be playing a huge role in supporting the Australian-Indian agenda of highlighting the business sectors of both the countries and the vibrant roles being played by both of them therewith. The key role of the Australia-India Business Champions Group is to liberalise and strengthen the bilateral trade between both the countries to be able to together pave the way to a collaborative economic growth, as has been quoted by Mr. Dan Tehan, the Australian Minister of Trade, Tourism, and Investment (Press Information Bureau, Government of India, 2021).

1.5. What Includes Critical Technologies?

The emergence of the COVID-19 pandemic upon the wide globe has made a number of nations realise their unhealthy dependence upon the wrong sources of supply chains, as has also been elucidated in the previous section. What matters even more is the development and progress towards a state of Globalisation 5.0, for which a sturdy form of technology drive is required, keeping in mind that China has been the superpower and an emerging hegemon in this context (United Nations Statistics Division, 2000). For the Indo-Pacific to become a more reliable spot for the beneficial interest of geopolitics to shift towards, the region has to look towards establishing competent technologies which outpowers the Chinese influence.

In order to become self-sufficient in nature, countries have to look towards bettering their resilience on supply chains and critical technologies respectively. However, for the latter, a considerable production of rare earth is required, 80% of which is extracted in China, thus reigning a monopoly over the mineral. India is at a beneficial stage along with Australia considering their agreement, since it is considered to be the second largest supplier of rare earths, i.e., approximately 11% of the total world's production, especially after the country realised its potential to become the top supplier of cobalt and zircon to India (Bachhawat, et al., 2020).

Due to the raging COVID-19 pandemic and its negative influence on various domestic economies, several nations have started looking towards inward looking policy formulation which would ultimately benefit their own countries (Sharma, et al., 2021). Due to the distrust of a range of major economies and trade wars amongst each other in the past two years, a sense of technological rivalry has also emerged which intends to benefit only a specific country's interest, rather than the whole globe, or even a cluster of countries situated in a region. An example of this could be the Chinese influence on the Asia-Pacific which ultimately translated into strategies which majorly benefit the Chinese economy itself.

This state of affairs has been even more exacerbated due to the presence of the United States' extremely apparent reluctance towards maintaining its customary leadership position in regards to the institutions which supported the American role in support and globalisation. Thus, this state of affairs further promotes a stage of a multifarious suspension of globalisation. In this context, major nation states who previously vouched for globalisation by achieving critical infrastructure such as telecommunication venders who are preparing to partner up with 5G are presently considering where these vendors come from, what are their supply chains, and what international behaviour do they resort to.

Although it is apparent from the previous state of strong and reliable set of global supply chains, most countries across the globe have transformed from technology takers towards the path of becoming technologically makers for their own benefit, as is also in line with inward looking policy formulation. Factors such as consequences of technological governance, civil rights, geopolitics, data protection and privacy, national security, ethics, and trust have become more important than the mere factor of cost effectiveness, during the process of the formulation of national strategies and policy formulation (Bachhawat, et al., 2020).

The emergence of the COVID-19 pandemic has realised several worthy partnerships amongst nations who can uplift the current state of affairs into better possibilities, simply by adhering to healthier protocols in regards to supply chain initiatives. The pandemic, in this sense, has not only hampered the lifestyle and standard of living, but it has also played a huge role in helping the world realise its extreme dependency on a sole source for technological advancement, i.e., the Chinese influence. Due to this, many such partnerships have emerged between countries which promote self-reliance and inward looking policies and development. One such partnership that may be quoted is of India and Australia, both of which have allied together to find advanced and high-tech manufacturing powers amongst themselves.

In this context, while India strives to become a global manufacturing hub to ultimately become the most reliable source of a global supply chain, Australia receives better access to the effective base of India's cost-effective, talented, and efficient labour and supplies. Similarly, India also benefits from the Australian industries in this context since the main issue of re-igniting critical technologies can be solved if the most important elements of critical technologies, i.e., supply rare earths is encountered. Since Australia has a natural supply of this key element, the agreement between Australia and India to cooperate in order to form self-reliant critical technologies, it reflects a growing synergy with a strong relationship between the two countries in the future, as the same also supports India's prime 'Make in India' and 'Aatmanirbhar Bharat' programmes (Bachhawat, et al., 2020). Thus, through these methods, India has gained an upper hand in being able to establish an Indo-centric approach towards the possibility of Indo-Pacific in the strategic and critical technologies sector, by partnering up with Australia in a bilateral cooperation while continuing their investments on strategic technology sectors. Moreover, in the June 2020 virtual summit between the prime ministers of both the countries, i.e., Shri Narendra Modi and Mr. Scott Morrison, had signed an agreement in relation to cyber and critical technologies where both the countries agreed to cooperate and collaborate with each other to ensure a healthy and self-reliant future (Burton, 2020).

In this context, India has successfully been able to carve a path of being an emerging technological hub of the globe, while being quoted as a leading and reliable source of IT services (Bachhawat, et al., 2020). In addition to this, Australia has achieved a favourable first-mover advantage in making efficient, effective, and sensitive technology related policies for a long term strategy. An example of this can be the Australian banning of high risk vendors in 2018, which led to China's Huawei and ZTE being effectively banned from its 5G network. Similarly, India has its own share in banning Chinese counterparts, such as barring the state owned telecommunication companies from using Chinese 5G equipment after the incident of Galwan (Bachhawat, et al., 2020).

1.6. What Constitutes the Liberal Rules-Based Order?

The concept of the "liberal" rules-based order, in a generalist sense, for the purposes of this report, has the following components:

- That it is inspired by the value systems of liberalism & the contemporary principles and practices of neoliberal school of thought, in policy;
- That rules and regulatory behaviour in multilateral institutions/forums and via multilateral treaties must quantify, in experience, action and operation, according to the principles and practices of liberalism;
- That the state of order must be comprehended and sought through the lens of the neoliberal school of thought, in various avenues of policy;

Of course, schools of thought need to materialise in action, which can lead to more honest and pragmatic impact assessments, to criticise and understand how the ontological basis works. In the case of the "**liberal**" rules-based order, as a concept in principle and practice, it is clearly visible that countries in various geopolitical constructs try to emanate their perspectives on the order and the liberal ontology, which has driven the transformation of international law, and liberal internationalism. For the Indo-Pacific, the commitments placed by countries do try to reconcile with the libertarian view of Free and Open Indo-Pacific, of one of the chief proponents of the Indo-Pacific concept, the United States (Observer Research Foundation, 2021). The European Union recently came up with a much reconciling perspective of ideation on this concept, considering both India and Pakistan as important stakeholders in the Indo-Pacific region (European Commission, 2021). It is therefore becoming clear that various countries, including certain important stakeholders, like India & the European Union have started engaging on establishing the diplomatic confines of what must deliberately constitute the liberal rules-based order. There is no doubt that as the exchange of such perspectives is done among governments across the globe, there will be certain principled commonalities. However, ideological commitments towards the school of neoliberalism are not so strong, which is because of the multipolar nature of the realpolitik. The United States has been the larger ideological source behind the rules-based order conception, and has even shaped concepts of war, peace, international law and other notions of global governance, for its own diplomatic convenience and other reasons (Stahl, 2021; Jr., 2006; Pant, 2021).

The use of the term liberalism for the Indo-Pacific also involves the indication of what coherent and incoherent diplomatic positions countries who are interested in the region would arise, followed by avenues of cooperation and resistance by various countries. **Multipolarity** in the current context ensures that the economics, ontology and promise of liberalism would become more decentralised and slower than before, considering the rise of middle powers across the globe (for example, India, Turkey, China and others).

For India, the important challenges in terms of committing to preserve multilateral institutions stem from the multipolar nature of the geopolitical situation, which — considering India's much balanced and adaptive foreign policy positions, would be helpful. India's positions will become mature and pragmatic and not ideological, as they were, under its earlier commitment to the policy of non-alignment. How will India shape the notion of rules-based order, for the emerging economic situation in its own region, the central point of focus for the Indo-Pacific region, would shape India's diplomatic confines of liberalism.

1.7. What Constitutes Inclusion?

Inclusion as a term can mean many things. For a better estimate, there can be layers of stakeholders, who can be in a hierarchical fashion of priority, be set up, to inspect to analyse what can constitute inclusion. For the Indo-Pacific region, India would commonly seek its "**inclusion**" strategies in a multidisciplinary manner, on the basis of three important trends:

- How the public policy realities which affect the internal economies and societies, should be taken into consideration, autonomously?

- How and what kinds of parameters can be developed for the Indo-Pacific as a region itself, looking at regions and their priorities?
- Does the infrastructure of "inclusion" really contribute towards those policy goals aimed by the countries, (especially India, for the purposes of this report)?

In general, the estimate of inclusion itself for the Indo-Pacific region, is either agnostic, absent, or ignored by countries, considering the specific contexts behind those goals, which shape how inclusion works. For the United States, countering the economic and armed presence of China is a concern, which many countries indirectly share with. For certain countries like India, the resilience and strength of domestic supply chains implies further inclusion of the MSMEs, be it services or manufacturing, within states and union territories. For some countries, inclusion might imply political inclusion of certain countries, increasing diplomatic ties with them, and transforming political/economic integration or cooperation with some countries accordingly. If the Indo-Pacific region is considered as a **focal moat** (i.e., an indirect political construct to shape priorities of the developed & developing countries in collaboration) to transform plurilateral and multilateral means of global governance, then India can act as a **neutral power** to serve the focal transformation of the region, in much wider terms. Of course, the trajectory of inclusion must not be regarded as merely on ideological or idealistic terms, but must be rooted on providing consensus of **national/local considerations and the emerging global trends**.

1.8. What Constitutes Commitment to Global Governance and Multilateralism?

India is a special proponent of multilateralism, where its policy of "reformed multilateralism" (Ministry of External Affairs, Government of India, 2020; Ministry of External Affairs, Government of India, 2021b) is a reflection of these understandings:

- That India takes many idealist or moralist stances on reaffirming the better, pragmatic and responsible goals of multilateralism;

- Despite the fact that it represents the concerns of the developing economies, by, for example its actual participation in the early days of the UN Conference on Trade and Development in the 1950s-60s (Agarwal, 1983 pp. 447-462), India still is saturating the bargaining relationship between developing (and underdeveloped economies) and developing countries;
- India is one of the unique countries in the category of developing economies in Asia & Africa, which focuses on the role of cooperative and collaborative governance (Jha, 2022; Sridharan, 2022) and the need of entrepreneurship and strategic investments to transform the national economies (Shaw, 2020);

In practical terms, India's case is adaptive, for the Indo-Pacific region, and like China and some Asian countries, India also invests in infrastructure projects domestically, and beyond (Chaudhary, 2018; Sinha, 2017). In many ways, India's dire commitment to global governance and multilateralism is subject to transformation.

As far as **government-to-government (G2G) engagement** is concerned, India has ambitious domestic infrastructure initiatives, with its own common problems any developing economy or a **Global South** country would face, as far as India's political economy is concerned. Internationally, India's financial and infrastructure support has to shift from being symbolic to become long-run, as it is known that countries, such as Turkey & China in Africa and the United States of America & the European Union countries in Eastern Europe have invested in various infrastructure projects. The challenges are not too rapid, but are similar ones, where questions related to the sustainability of such investments, financial assistance and projects must be raised. India in general has much **diplomatic goodwill globally**, and its cooperation with the United States must be seen **specifically**, in this regard. However, the translation of such goodwill into state capacity which empowers the Indian Government to wield its influence and even strategic existentialism cum presence in the conceived Indo-Pacific region, remains to be seen. With the United States too, it is yet to be seen if partnerships in various areas, at various levels, and so, through multiple actors, would empower India, or not. The United States simply matters here because it is one of India's **largest involved partner** (Jaishankar, 2021). The United Kingdom is the **next country** after the US, but the US wields more importance in the same regard.

Now, in the present case, the most critical portion of the Indo-Pacific region, is the one including India, commonly known as the South Asian Region (SAR) (or the Indian Subcontinent), due to a variety of reasons. The West Indian Ocean region, ranging up to South and East Africa does add up too, due to the maritime reasons and the trade considerations involved. In the SAR, India would attempt to internationalise its engagement with the international community, including the US, the UK, , the Arab states, the EU countries and even the ASEAN member-states. The **United States** is playing an important role in shaping India's foreign policy approaches, because of the following reasons:

- US companies (and even civil societies/NGOs) have strategic investments within India, shaping the sluggish nature of India's political economy (impact might vary sector-wise and entity-wise);
- Indian and American stakeholders in various domains are subject to and undergoing projects and initiatives in collaboration;
- It is yet to be seen how the Indian counterparts are benefiting and developing their strategic measures to strengthen the potential and plausibility as a critical actor in the Indo-Pacific region;
- The US-China relations and their disruptive repercussions seem to much influence discourses and even policy designs of the Indian counterparts, whether at the level of the Union Government, or the companies and rest of the multiple stakeholders;
- India still has not achieved parity to transform reasonable avenues of autonomous transformation in its

policy designs, due to the ill-effects of the repercussions caused by US-China relations. There should be structural considerations involved;

In the case of certain older partners and stakeholders, in Eurasia, India however has established and transformed avenues of cooperation (for example, Saudi Arabia, UAE, Russia, Japan, DPRK and others). Also, for India, since reformed multilateralism is going to become an essential imperative, it has to be materialised, and not limited to symbolic activities to show moral diplomatic gestures. This therefore makes it imperative to question India's global governance methodology per se. It does not mean there is no capability, or the Union Government lacks any potential. The problem lies in yet structuring India's infrastructure priorities.

1.9. What Includes Strategic Autonomy?

India's strategic autonomy has been very conditionally ingrained with the Cold War period of the 1960s, and since the liberalisation in the 1990s, its inclination towards the United States has shaped its strategic autonomy widely. India's strategic autonomy is however also shaped by how it looks at the relationship between the policy constructs based on the principles of multilateralism, and those on the basis of the realpolitik that plurilateralism offers. India's moralism helps in maintaining itself as a different policy actor in the Indo-Pacific either through its sovereign representation or through its consistency of support towards the multilateral institutions. However, that still does not complete India's strategic autonomy architecture, because it has to be incentivised and designed through proper economic and security paradigms cum priorities.

In an increasingly multipolar world, where the system of allies is being replaced by strategic, natural and tactical partnerships between the big and middle powers, not merely similarly in all sectors of industry, development & defence, but quite much in a diversified fashion, India, despite its reinforced statements after statements that it seems to be "non-aligned" is pursuing the policy of multi-alignment as

according to S Akbaruddin, India's former Permanent
Representative at the United Nations (Akbaruddin, 2021;
Akbar, 2019). India's approach towards BRICS, SCO and the
Russia-India-China triad reflects a clear internal policy of
multi-alignment, which, of course can be named as "non-
alignment" (O'Donnell, et al., 2021 pp. 801-822). Also, as the
Indian counterparts via government officials, civil society,
entrepreneurs, scholars, professionals and even people from
the diasporas and communities have interacted with those of
the US and the rest of the "West", there are increasing signs
of pragmatic cooperation – which is to state, cooperation
based on realities and constraints, and not just value systems.
For example, the American legal and administrative
infrastructure, certainly has several flaws, and so cannot be
juxtaposed in any form of policy imagination in India, by any
stretch of imagination. Reasons are clear that India's
constitutional and policy priorities require India to become a
state with a strong Union/Central Government, with more
empowerment to the District-level authorities and
democratic constituencies. Imagining a policy reform model
for a post-colonial India, whose constitutional and
administrative reforms, pragmatically, has to be seen from a
complete Indian outlook, with some global observations, and
learnings to at least foresee consequential impact, and avoid
any major policy lapse.

In that proper sense, India's strategic autonomy cannot be
isolated as to be stated as merely "US-Centric", "China-
Centric", "Pro-Russia" or merely "Quad-led". Phrasal
keywords like these do reflect affinity or repulsion towards
any geopolitical grouping or actor, whether in the domain of
hard power or of the soft power. It therefore is not simple to
assume that India requires an ally system. C Raja Mohan
claims that India has had an alliance system in some way,
where he cites the 1971 India-Pakistan war, where the USSR
had supported India (Mohan, 2021) against the US Navy, and
in many occasions, the Russians have been helpful in vetoing
UNSC draft resolutions against India's national interest.
While the proposition merits fairly, that simply happened
because India's NAM policy was incomplete and deprived of
any domestic and transnational priorities. In that realm,

India's neutrality as a foreign policy tool per se, cannot be exactly compared with those of Switzerland or Norway.

2 Assessing the Anatomy of Policy Challenges for India: Proposals and Analyses

In this section of the report, we have proposed a policy proposal which pivots India as the key player in shaping global governance for the Indo-Pacific, to begin with.

2.1. The Extent and Aspects

For the purposes of this work, it is responsible and necessary to define the scope of usage of the term, "Indo-centrism". The term is proposed for the purposes of this report, which specifically means, that India requires to shape its priorities and interests to form its polity, with domestic and transnational potential, which by all means, is not just central to India's interests, but also productive to India's domestic and local aspirations cum realities. Indo-centrism is a policy proposal, which signifies how India can conceive the Indo-Pacific, under two important aspects of understandability, which are mentioned as follows:

- India-based
- Indo-Europeanism

The term **India-based** implies here that India's foreign policy and domestic policy priorities must benefit and expand India's interests and purpose as a significant power in the Indian subcontinent region/the Indian Ocean region in the Indo-Pacific construct. The term **Indo-Europeanism** is often associated with the Indo-European languages and the similarities in the Indian and European cultures, which range from Central and Eastern Europe to the Indian subcontinent. The term can also be related with the geography of Eurasia, where older civilisations in India, Russia, Persia, Arabia, China and even continental Europe were deeply connected through several land routes. In the present context, India can be assumed as a central middle power in the Indo-Pacific construct, where as its Act East policy compels it to expand strategic and economic engagement with East Asian countries in South East Asia and even countries like Japan. However, India's cultural and historical relationship with Europe can be more deeply related with the Greco-Roman culture, than colonialism of the British Empire. The role of West Asia is also considered important here, considering India's ever-engaging relations with the West Asian countries like Israel, Palestine, Saudi Arabia, UAE and even Egypt, for example. If we look north, then India's engagement with the Central Asian countries and even the members of the Shanghai Cooperation Organisation, makes the level of engagement, at the level of Eurasia as a whole.

2.2. Examining and Revisiting Global and Liberal Constructivism

The term 'constructivism' emerged as a saviour of the systems of international paradigms in place of liberalism and realism, during the end of the Cold War. Constructivism was first coined by Nichloas Onuf in his celebrated book of World of Our Making, wherein the term defined the importance of roles and identities being defined in accordance with social practices of the respective countries (Onuf, 2013). Through this ideology, it was rationalised that defining identities would allow states to define their core interests, through which their actions, needs, and goals may be predicted (Wetering, 2018 pp. 57-80). However, it is imperative to note, in accordance with the neo-liberal and neo-realist school of thought, material forces do not a play a role in defining a state's identities or beliefs.

As the post-colonial era emerged, the eastern bloc of countries which includes the countries involved in the Indo-Pacific and the ASEAN corridors regained their indigenous political philosophy which further helped them to develop their own set of theories about security and sovereignty (Mignolo, 2017 pp. 39-45). However, with time, as the western influence grew stronger in power, they gained an unfair tool of being able to alter the interests of states respectively in their own self-righteous interest. Herein, came about the infamous problem with the coloniality of knowledge, i.e., the ontology of North Atlantic's Universal Fictions has convinced us to believe in terms of being able to appear 'superiorly' in knowledge as compared to the eastern bloc of countries (Trouillt, 2002 pp. 839-858; Chatterjee, 1993). As the emerging powers of the eastern bloc countries grew stronger, mainly in China, India, and Brazil, the phenomenon came to a bumpy halt in the beginning of the 21st century. As the respective countries thus coming in power desperately searched for their lost set of indigenous knowledge, they realised that they were fed pretentious notions of a colonial hegemony, i.e., brainwashed by the western influence (Mignolo, 2017; Ikenberry, 2010).

India, in particular, along with other countries involved in the corridors of the ASEAN and the Indo-Pacific, is of the strong view that colonial powers have contributed to immensely demoting the social capacities of India in the context of science and technological aspects, as claimed. Moreover, it is also contended that the country's ancient legacies have been ignored which has made the country weak in stone and unable to grasp power until independence. Any such place which had the hands of colonialism in their recent history has realised the same is marked with dark spots, i.e., certain closed policy narratives that simply do not emanated into policy narratives of national interest of the respective countries (Bauman, 2011).

This highlights the importance of realizing that the western narrative has taught independent countries to have a selective memory, while still having an indirect power over their lands through the concept of unipolarity (Hobsbawm, et al., 1983). In other words, the colonial power was able to affect the multipolar nature of the realpolitik, however, only till the beginning of the 21st century. This translates into the fact that the Indian approach to smooth policy formulation simply for some time has been defeatist and unclear, simply because of severe structural and operative problems in defining India's strategic autonomy doctrines, which reflects not just in the realms of strategic affairs and foreign policy, but also in cultural policy, public law, technology policy, education studies, economic policy and other fields in the realm of public policy. Moreover, according to the analysis of

Hofferberth and Weber, 'constructivism' essentially refers to the idea that rules cannot be based on assumptions, where since facts are not scientifically driven, cannot be depended upon either. Thus, they argued that the norms of social constructivism in International Theory must be constantly renegotiated in social interaction, the lack of which has resulted in a shift of colonial power (Hofferberth, et al., 2015 pp. 75–103).

2.3. The Adaptability and Manoeuvrability in the Position

It is important to state that India's potential to adapt and manoeuvre its priorities, potential and constraints in the domains of hard power and soft power, are subject to its core policy approaches and strategies, to shape its priorities, develop its potential and also overcome and cope up with the constraints in place. India, since is a large economy, with a huge internal market and definitely is shaping its security priorities reasonably, would have to take an **incremental** approach to deal with its realities and shape the environments of diplomatic, economic and political engagement in the international community, accordingly. Lack of clarity towards state-centrism is why India cannot adopt a short-run model to shape its priorities.

2.4. Policy Consequentialism: Extent and Pragmatism

In general, the consequence of a policy, for the purposes of this report, for a nation-state or a civilisation, in historical terms, can be designated in 2 ways. One consequence can be that it is **linear**, where once the act ends, the second and third order effects of a policy event remain to reveal but the end point of that policy action/omission has anyways unavoidably reached. Otherwise, it may be possible that the consequences of a policy event do not lead to the end of the policy event's relevance, existence and influence, but is a rather stemmed continuation of the same in ethos and practice, which is like a cycle in a continuous motion without friction. Now, nations or civilisations can have 2 more states of policy consequence otherwise, apart from the 2 described. Those states are called the **Helical** and **Null** states.

The Helical state signifies that a subtle and closely planned combination of policy measures, of both linear and cyclic nature, can create a state helical policy consequence, where a policy event's continuous nature leads to its existence, while the event shapes itself as its linear components grow and decay with time. A null state is simply the state of nullity, i.e., nothing happens nor anything is acted upon in the field of policy.

Thinkers like Sri Aurobindo, Swami Vivekananda and others, have signified that India represents a civilisation of continuity in their works on spirituality, nationhood and ethics (Aurobindo, 1997 pp. 188, 207-209, 288). Even in policy paradigms, prominent thinkers of the 20th century in India, especially those who contributed to India's national independence movement, shared this view that India, clearly **is continuous in its transformation** as far as its cultural and civilisational heritage is concerned. In fact, extensive research is being conducted by the Government of India and several institutions like the Indian Institutes of Technology in Kharagpur, Mumbai (Bombay), Chennai (Madras) and others in the field of **Indic Knowledge Systems/Indian Knowledge Systems (IKS),** with special multidisciplinary focus in natural, special and applied sciences to rejuvenate and seek better policy and core ideas and concepts which accord with the traditional knowledge that comes with assets of India's cultural heritage. The report thus does not speculate how the effort of IKS translates into India's foreign policy and diplomatic measures. However, it can be stated that the potential of standardizing and advancing Indian science — considering the capabilities of India's pharmaceutical industry (for example), might be helpful in shaping India's role as a middle power in the international community.

In reality, countries as nation-states whether through unilateral, plurilateral or multilateral measures — balance their linear and cyclic choices accordingly. India since represents **perennial connectivity and continuity**, clearly bears the potential to master both linear and cyclic policy approaches, shape its overall helical paradigm of development and growth, as a country. We therefore recommend in this work that India can approach its own **Helical** methods in policymaking and transformation as a clear and undoubted priority. In the further sections, we have provided some preliminary considerations with some illustrations on how can positive formulations be prepared in that regard.

3 Basis of the Indo-centric approach in Global Governance

This section of the report formulates some preliminary considerations in proposition needed to establish an Indo-centric approach in Global Governance.

3.1. Multi-Aligned Neutrality

During the Cold War period, India, Egypt, former Yugoslavia and Egypt had led the Non-Aligned Movement to propose and shape up a consistent alternative against the blocs led by the US and the USSR, and the history of colonialism and subjugation. In the 1950s, India had become an important member of the United Nations Conference on Trade And Development, to support the cause of the developing and underdeveloped economies across the globe. Assessing the complicated history of NAM clearly shows India's moral and balanced commitment to the earlier policy of non-alignment and even towards the cause of the developing and underdeveloped economies. We also know that models of state-level neutrality varies, and has its own layers of transformation. A policy of neutrality can be restricted or limited to a particular field, such as defence, economics & trade, political affairs, cultural policy and other relevant areas. In a multipolar realpolitik, in line with Professor John Mearsheimer's view of strategic autonomy (Strategic Studies Quarterly, 2018; Walt, 2018), the following aspects are to be understood:

- Multipolarity ensures that the systematic tendencies of forming ententes and alliances – which classically used to involve all-comprehensive cooperation, are discouraged by many means of human occurrence and actions. Since, the **bifurcation and specialization of soft power and hard power constructs has been made possible**, countries now opt for **strategic, tactical and natural partnerships**, subject to the areas of common interest, and not as a whole alongside;

- Multipolarity usually is considered a case where the global order is deeply anarchic, and completely obsessed with the power projections of emergent, middle and emerging powers. **Often some areas of interest may share similar policy incidents and tendencies, but they might vary distinctively,** and their combinations might affect the partner countries quite differently;

- Multipolarity since involves a case-to-case cooperation approach, **it becomes apparent that classical and neoliberal multilateral systems lack the capability to adapt and shape their policy relevance with time**. Organisations like the United Nations and its agencies too, for example, share the kind of policy paralysis, in the international arena;

- Multilateralism has its own value and purpose, and it is therefore important to realize that multipolarity of the global order shapes the construct of sovereignty by all means. **Like soft power and hard power, concepts like hard law and soft law become relevant**, where pseudo-states, conceptually – and to some extent, practically, become relevant. The tendencies of self-regulation of companies and even NGOs, can shape the global order, if sovereignty is not utilized effectively. It can be stated that **power politics does not limit to countries anymore, but also may extend to non-state actors**;

- In a multipolar order, there are two kinds of states in terms of **structural importance in the realpolitik – nation-states and civilisation-states**. While the legal estimate of a nation-state is clearly determinable, the **"persona ficta"** (Abhivardhan, et al., 2021a) or the **civilisation-state** is an **obscure merger** or **mix** of a nation-state with subject-wise potential non-state actors, of domestic or transnational/transregional presence, which further complicates the role of public international law. Maybe it does not affect private international law as **multifaceted engagement** is the pivot of this field. While, non-state actors may pretend to act like pseudo-states, they might **too reflect the tendency of nation-states as to how they influence**

the relevant non-state actors. In general, civilisation-states can be relatively compared with the concept of empires and kingdoms, in some regard and not all;

- Multipolarity forces governments to adopt multifaceted **risk-centric approaches in policy**. Unlike the classical approaches of treating risks of specific areas, in specific domains, the intersectional impact of two or more areas of policy has to be assessed very carefully. Risk-centricity can largely define the stability, existence and perpetuity of any policy construct at the level of governments across the globe;

- There are two key tendencies which have emerged in the 21st century, especially since the 2010s: **minilateralism and multi-alignment**. Countries tend to form smaller strategic groups, or forums, or apply the tools of plurilateralism (bilateralism, trilateralism and others), to create a web or cluster of partnerships across the globe, wherever possible. Both of the newer trends reflect the need to have risk-centric approaches in all kinds of policy, subject to the disruption and the risks that may emanate. Policy incidents can be helical, linear or cyclic, but how they are approached, clearly reflects how the web of partnerships of nation-states works;

Taking the aforementioned points into consideration, it is proposed that India can reflect itself as a **clearly neutral, multi-aligned power**. India's foreign policy reflects certain bemused and dislocated power and competence projections. Yet, it is clear that while the Union Government might still claim that India abides with the principles of non-alignment, it can still transform its **risk-centric multi-alignment tendency**, by all means. **Multi-alignment is not a political ideology, but a clear policy ethic**, which governments can use to shape their core interests and capacities with time. Under this supposed tendency, which India in general has been following for decades now, despite the newly emergent Indo-US and Indo-Israeli relations since the 1990s, amidst the maintained Indo-Russian ties despite the collapse of the Soviet Union, for example.

The key questions which multi-aligned countries like India, must ask, in policy are expressed as follows:

- What are the risks which emerge? Are the risks short-term or long-term?
- How should the risks be dealt – and how is it ensured that the risks are used to shape up the legal and policy matrices of the state?
- Considering that territorial and maritime sovereignty are areas of core interests ad infinitum, what special interests can be accepted and shaped with time?
- Is development pursued with a piecemeal approach, or the institutional approach, must share some space with the disruptions and the associated risks, to wield sufficient influence to shape development policies?

The key questions, which neutral countries like India must ask, in policy are expressed as follows:

- Does neutrality invite positive or negative restrictions on any sector or actor?
- Can a state be strategically open to foster and consumer cum absorb the disruptive tendencies of the policy incidents per se?
- Can neutrality exist for a state without being resourceful?

Specific recommendations have been provided at the end of the report. However, the determining factors in some key areas, have already been explained in the further portions.

3.2. Indian Approaches towards International Law and Global Governance

The essence of Indian interest may be described as a 'moralistic force' or an upcoming leader of the developing countries, i.e., the Third World. In fact, due to its obstructive nature, it has often been termed as an activist for the developmental issues of the third world, as was noted by Former Secretary General Kofi Annan (Anant, 2001 pp. 4243-4245; Dabhade, 2017). Annan also mentioned in his speech of 2005, that the UN agenda on behalf of the developing world has been largely influenced by the activism of India and its persistent objection. India's true ambition had always been to fulfil the long-standing goal of achieving the larger freedom, i.e., development, security, and guaranteed human rights to the developing and least-developed countries.

Thus, in most global collaborations, India has been known to have a flawed rejectionist approach, a remark which was picked up by numerous scholars as they went on to state that India does not simply engage in activism for the third world, but also uses the international institutions to its advantage, ultimately aiding the motives of the developing and least-developed countries (Anant, 2001; Narlikar, 2007). For example, in the troposphere of the global trading system, India recognized and ruled out that the system majorly reflected the interests of developed countries. In this context, a number of Indian ministers in a number of WTO ministerial conferences highlighted that the mechanisms of multilateral trading systems should not only serve the interests of developed countries, but all the signatories, with a focus on developing and least-developed countries (Sharma, et al., 2017).

However, the decade long obstructive nature of India saw a drastic change 2014 onwards, specifically in the Trade Facilitation Agreement that had emerged from Bali, wherein the country depicted business-friendly credentials, transforming from the champion of the third world, to a consensus-building emerging power (Sharma, et al., 2021). It is imperatively noted that India's true essence of standing by the needs of developing countries was still prominent but in a manner which did not persist the international negotiating table. This, however, did not result in any positive outcomes for the country, but rather pushed the nation deeper in the concerns of developing and least-developed countries (Kanth, 2016 pp. 44-50). In any case, the Indian ministers pursued this strategy in the national interest of achieving more foreign investment as well as for receiving a greater access to the markets of developed countries (Chanda, et al., 2007 pp. 169-213).

This was when India's essence started being taken more liberally, an act which was seen as a betrayal by its former alliances supporting the third world. It has always been clear that India's true interest shall be to change the international conundrum in such a manner that its reciprocities are beneficial to the developing and least-developed countries in a fair, equitable, and just manner (Sharma, et al., 2021). In this context, it must be observed that power and legitimacy in an individual sense do not have to be binary but may complement each other in order to avail 'the good country's equation' (Anholt, 2020; Bommakanti, 2017). However, amongst legitimacy, a political dimension must also be catered to, wherein the political leaders are able to comprehend the function of legitimization. This is because, it has been often quoted by learned scholars in the realm of philosophy that political leaders in a country are more concerned about the approval of other states, rather than their own foreign policy decisions that they can make independent of any external influence (Claude, 1996 pp. 367-379).

However, in recent times, as the geopolitical tensions between countries rise and the American unipolarity stands on its verge, India has decided to uplift its international profile and capabilities, by shifting from the position of a 'rule taker' to a 'rule maker.' The sole Indian acts of forming an alliance with regimes like the Missile Technology Control Regime (MTCR) and the Nuclear Supplier's Group (NSG) translate into the fact that the state will not be satisfied by being the target of larger powers or by being followers of other international powers (Dabhade, 2017).

3.3. Indigenization and Indianizing Systems

Often it is proposed that India requires to indigenize and "Indianise" its policy priorities. Indianization clearly means to make policy priorities India-centric. Often this is proposed by scholars and policymakers in India, that to Indianize means to adopt certain policy considerations of the past, of certain empires and kingdoms, in the Indian subcontinent or to merely assume to domesticate certain policy considerations (Abhivardhan, et al., 2021b). Now – there is no doubt that Indianizing is possible. There are certain clear policy undertakings, which belong India's rich cultural heritage and history. How they work out in the real-time contexts would largely shape their relevance, and so, it becomes important that Indianization should not be limited to merely acting as imitators of change, but as the designers of change. Policy designs require proper substantive backing, in any discipline. In order to see where Indianization is possible, India's knowledge economy requires many economic, pedagogical and structural reforms. It is also required that holistic tendencies towards shaping quality of life and sustainable development, are discovered, tested, proven and then adopted with time. Cultural diplomacy works when the **economics of sustainability & development is cultivated**. Without the same, mere moralistic gestures and policy promises do not help out, which leads to the accidental adoption of counterproductive policy ideas, which are usually poorly planned out.

4 Determining Policy Consequentialism for India

In this section, the policy proposal as described and proposed, has been backed with analysis on the nodes of operability and purpose, which can contribute in making the policy proposal of Indo-centrism clear and pragmatic.

4.1. The Indo-European Motivation within Indo-centrism

In generic terms, the Indo-Pacific, like the erstwhile Asia-Pacific and Euro-Atlantic conceptions, is a **piecemeal construct**, to shape the future of global governance, considering the subtle fact that Asia, as a critical part of the Eurasian continental area, is set to gain large importance in terms of technology democratisation, climate cum maritime security, knowledge economy and other relevant matters of interest. Recently, the 4th Quad Summit of 2022 was concluded in Melbourne, Australia (Office of the Spokesperson, 2022), in which several geopolitical, economic and diplomatic issues were addressed. As compared to the othered objective for which the Quadrilateral, as we know, was upgraded, and shaped since 2017, it seems that there are some serious issues with the minilateral forum, which reflects fault lines in the Indo-US relations as well as the US Foreign Policy visions per se, which are enumerated as follows:

- The Quad members are taking too many policy issues in the Indo-Pacific, where some of them are too distracting, or unclear. There also exist some new policy issues in due suggestion, which are too impractical to be even implemented;

- The Quad is not monopolizing or mastering specific policy issues of short-term interest to crystallise the Indo-Pacific strategic visions that all the four countries keep up with. For example, India through its Vaccine Maitri initiative delivered many vaccines as a matter of humanitarian support to many Global South countries, which the rest of the Quad countries unfortunately did not, in 2021. The relevance of vaccine distribution can be questioned distinctively, but the approaches have been confused in many ways, in general, which the Quad members have not addressed properly;

- The Quad is too passive and does not offer institutional support to India, the most active and important regional power, in the Indo-Pacific region, as far as its comparison with the rest of the Quad members is properly done. Lack of clarity in leading institutionalization, especially from countries like the United States, despite India's eager and interest, must raise important questions of policy and diplomacy, as far as the purpose of the Quad is concerned;

As discussed before, stating that an Indo-Pacific approach whether is anti-China, or pro-US, or anything within some binary political or ideological undertaking, would be somewhere unsustainable, because the relevance of interests and approaches in a multipolar order, would surely change the inclinations behind whatsoever countries regard as the Indo-Pacific. According to media reports, India does not consider Ukraine a part of the geography of the Quad countries (Chaudhary, 2022) and differed with the US on Myanmar as well, clearly indicating that India's Act East policy and its Indo-Pacific outlook are **pragmatic and not ideological/doctrinal**. It has been clear that India, despite claiming it follows non-alignment per se, has completely shaped its **institutional vision of non-alignment, and its doctrinal vision of strategic autonomy**. The conception of non-alignment under former Indian PM Nehru was clearly ideological, idealist and philosophical. The legacy of that approach decayed with time, and since the end of the Cold War and India's liberalization in the 1990s, India has opened up to the international community, quite uniquely, despite its defeatist and confused tendencies in the past. Clearly, the post-colonial effect that the Indian foreign policy still suffers from is transitioning smoothly, and India is **now becoming a trusted rule-maker, beyond just a rule-taker**.

As it has been stated, Indo-centrism has two key elements, i.e., it has to be India-based and must retain to be Indo-

European. Beyond geography and cultural history, the element of Indo-Europeanism can be considered as an **element of stability**, in expanding the **capital of multilateral institutions, initiatives & forums and plurilateral measures of India's interest and concern**. The following points describe the extent of the Indo-European motivation:

- India can foster the existing multilateral institutions, and address their systemic issues. However, if necessary, India can propose and invest in creating better and reliable multilateral institutions. A neutral power like India can shape its notions of governance, state sovereignty, institutional credibility, and other emerging conceptions of international law, which are **incremental and deeply rooted in the realities of the Indo-European/Eurasian geography**. India's stakes are imperative in the Indian Ocean region as well as in the Eurasian landmass, which can direct India's ambitions, and stabilize its methodology, which is **helical** in nature. We are confident to propose that this deep-rooted motivation can enhance India's commitment and interest in **reformed multilateralism** as we know it;

- India as a multi-aligned power will have to require immense diplomatic, armed, economic and technological capacities to keep itself at bay as the multi-polar tendencies of the global order shape with time, so that it germinates and strengthens its **issue-based partnerships** with countries of **strategic/tactical/natural purpose**. The loop of issue-based partnerships can make India more experienced with any fermenting global risks that regularly emerge with time. Risks shape countries' sovereign decisions, and so India has to increase its activity to see where partnerships can be made, or partnerships, if possible, can be **converted** into **potential alliances/ententes**. Here – the significance of the Eurasian geography can make India quite **pragmatic and resilient**, as it intends to advance itself more to the East. It can give India to use multilateral initiatives as strategic mcats to shape its long-term approach of existence and influence as the Indo-Pacific construct becomes a normative construct, like that of the Euro-Atlantic or the erstwhile Asia-Pacific;

The Eurasian geography has been central to India's policy transformation as a nation-state and a civilisation-state as we know it. Recognizing that the Eurasian geography is of larger value to India makes it more open to shape its relationship with **Europe, East Asia and Africa**, quite significantly. It may also enable India to pick and choose where, for example, it can expand and invest in, be it disruptive technology, sustainability, infrastructure projects or anything else. Now, for example, continental Europe (and not necessarily the European Union) and South East Asia (and not necessarily the Association of South East Asian Nations) can **shape diverse and decentralized approaches of strategic hedging** (Vennet, et al., 2019 pp. 86–134), like **India** (Kumar, 2019). To add, even countries in West Asia, especially Israel, Egypt, UAE, Saudi Arabia and Bahrain, can do the same, and shape more plurilateral efforts of cooperation with India, Europe and East Asia per se. The geography therefore can be used to distribute and mitigate several risks which the realpolitik in general offers. It certainly is a different question how middle powers look at it. However, India's experience in Eurasia is certainly nuanced, which inspires us to propose the Indo-European motivation.

4.2. India-led ASEAN-centricity

We propose that ASEAN-centricity (or ASEAN-centrality) must be India-led and India-based. Taking the first element of Indo-centrism, India must usher reasonable involvement in East Asia, as a **maritime power**. The focus on ASEAN for India must be largely inclined towards pragmatic issues of **environment and maritime security**. The members of the Quad in some ways do recognize the potential and clear role of India as a maritime power.

4.3. Power-Legitimacy Dynamics

As a **neutral power**, India can focus on enhancing its role in legal policy and international law, especially in dispute resolution, by improving its regulatory ecosystem internally, which require immense **compliance reforms** (Chikermane, et al., 2022). Indian courts and lawyers can contribute to India's steer focus to become an important hub of ADR mechanisms. There is no doubt that neutrality for India, is to be backed through proper **strategic hedging** that may challenge it at the first place. Another way to look at shaping and enhancing India's commitment as a neutral power, can be India's rule of law approach, points on which are enumerated as follows:

- The multipolar nature of the global order would eventually force countries globally, especially in the emerging Indo-Pacific construct to look through and contribute in strengthening the administrative and judicial institutions to **mitigate horizontal and vertical risks** caused due to **failure/irrationality in compliance or the utilization of judgments**. Addressing risks and the consistency of procedures established by law, would readily enhance the trust in Indian institutions. It might be a **state-based issue too**, which is subject to the regulations of various states & union territories across India;

- Instead of adopting top-down legal arguments to alter or create understandings on any emanating rights, liabilities and responsibilities, which is deprived of or justified through accurate policy analyses, **decentralized methods can be adopted** at the level of the Union Government, where perhaps the Ministry of Co-Operation if possible can look into;

- India needs mass-level upskilling and inclusion of legal professionals, wherein their role must not limit to mere litigation and law firm-related work. There are **several legal recourses, beyond and within the framework of alternate dispute resolution**, which can be gradually encouraged for the young population of law graduates to ensure that they do not limit themselves to limited legal career choices. For example, arbitration can become as a dedicated and distinctive career as compared to just practising as an advocate in any Court of law (Internationalism Global Podcasts, 2022);

- In multiple legal-economic fields, like intellectual property law, law & regulation technologies, investment law, corporate governance and others, cooperation can be established between India and various actors, on issues-based consensus established accordingly. We suggest that two important elements of cooperation can make these **issues-based legal cooperation** viable for India, when **(a) the economic rationale is settled, is productive, clear and eases India's cooperation in regulatory affairs between the administrative bodies and the courts; and (b) the retrospective and prospective issues with respect to cooperation are gradually alleviated**. However, it does not mean that easing down regulations clearly means to accept unfair legal, economic and trade cooperation. The **resilience** of national and local entities would support the Indian economy, and so it becomes important that the **domesticated calibration** of India's economic and regulatory outlooks improves to bargain for issues-based legal cooperation and is deep-rooted in sensibility, so that future decisions can address **(a) any foreign or internal disruptions (economic, technological, etc.,) along with the associated risks; and (b) the institutionalization of risk-based governance measures in general**;

The frugal nature of the Indian economy, especially the service sector, and the knowledge economy – which is intertwined with the technology ecosystems around the globe, raise bars of vulnerability against India's administrative and judicial capacity. While resourcefulness is a dire need, compliance must achieve clarity, purpose and sustainability.

5 Conclusion

The report does not provide any direct recommendations, since the intent of the authors has been to provide substantive legal and policy solutions and reflections. We conclude that if India aspires to lead the agenda of global governance in the Indo-Pacific, it has to be Indo-European and India-based. India can become a neutral power and address the natural risks of the multi-polar global order under its policy ethic of multi-alignment as sought. We understand that middle powers have compulsions and estimating direct correlations of the outcomes of any issues-based partnerships/alliance is not possible due to the heterogenous global risks, which middle powers like India, would naturally face. We however insist that India must adopt and shape its Indo-Pacific vision, which is not sublimed into any notion of pre-decided alliances with any state. Instead of values-based cooperation, which has severe fault lines, and is ideological, unclear and unsustainable, India must cultivate its multi-alignment policy ethic gradually. We insist that this report, along with the technical report **TR-002**, can serve as important sources of understanding for future technical reports which would focus on legal and policy solutions related to the Indo-Pacific. We are of the humblest view that institutional reforms and **strategic hedging** will help India achieve its goals in the Indo-Pacific construct, and we look forward to future contributions to the issue of India's contributions and role in the Indo-Pacific, in terms of global governance.

References

Observer Research Foundation. 2021. Partnership for a rules-based order in the Indo-Pacific. *Observer Research Foundation.* [Online] 6 September 2021. [Cited: 24 December 2021.] https://www.orfonline.org/research/partnership-for-a-rules-based-order-in-the-indo-pacific/.

European Commission. 2021. EU Strategy for Cooperation in the Indo-Pacific . *European External Action Service.* [Online] 16 September 2021. [Cited: 24 December 2021.] https://eeas.europa.eu/headquarters/headquarters-homepage_en/96740/EU%20Strategy%20for%20Cooperation%20in%20the%20Indo-Pacific.

Stahl, Daniel. 2021. Confronting US imperialism with international law. Central America and the arms trade of the inter-war period. *Journal of Modern European History.* 2021, Vol. 19, 4.

Jr., Ostergard, Robert L. 2006. The Failure of America's Post–Cold War Foreign Policy: From the Persian Gulf to the Gulf of Guinea. *The Whitehead Journal of Diplomacy and International Relations.* 2006.

Pant, Harsh, V. 2021. Biden's foreign policy lacks strategic clarity. *Observer Research Foundation.* [Online] 11 February 2021. [Cited: 24 December 2021.] https://www.orfonline.org/research/bidens-foreign-policy-lacks-strategic-clarity/.

Akbaruddin, Syed. 2021. Beyond Quad, the quest for multi-alignment. *Hindustan Times.* [Online] 20 September 2021. https://www.hindustantimes.com/opinion/beyond-quad-the-quest-for-multialignment-101632140166284.html.

Akbar, M. J. 2019. From non-alignment to multi-alignment. *Open.* [Online] 23 August 2019. https://openthemagazine.com/special/modis-foreign-policy-from-non-alignment-to-multi-alignment/.

O'Donnell, Frank and Papa, Mihaela. 2021. India's multi-alignment management and the Russia–India–China (RIC) triangle. *International Affairs.* 2021, Vol. 97, 3.

Mohan, C. Raja. 2021. Non-Alignment, nationalism and the Quad . *Observer Research Foundation.* [Online] 13 April 2021. https://www.orfonline.org/expert-speak/non-alignment-nationalism-and-the-quad/.

Hyome, K. 2020. 'ASEAN centrality' and the emerging great power competition. *Observer Research Foundation.* [Online] 2020. https://www.orfonline.org/expert-speak/asean-centrality-and-the-emerging-great-power-competition/.

Acharya, Amitava. 2017. The Myth of ASEAN Centrality. *Contemporary Southeast Asia.* 2017, Vol. 39.

—. 2014. *Constructing a Security Community in Southeast Asia: ASEAN and the Problem of Regional Order.* New York : Routledge, 2014.

Kraft, Herman Joseph. 2011. Driving East Asian Regionalism: The Reconstruction of ASEAN's Identity. [ed.] Ralf Emmers. *ASEAN and the Institutionalization of East Asia.* New York and London : Routledge, 2011.

Siddiqui, Huma. 2019. India's concept of Indo-Pacific is inclusive and across oceans. *Ministry of External Affairs, Government of India.* [Online] 2019. https://www.mea.gov.in/articles-in-indian-media.htm?dtl/32015/Indias_concept_of_IndoPacific_is_inclusive_and_across_oceans.

Heiduk, Felix and Wacker, Gudrun. 2020. From Asia-Pacific to Indo-Pacific: Significance, Implementation and Challenges. *German Institute for International and Security Affairs, Research Paper No. 9.* 2020.

Hemmings, John. 2018. Global Britain in the Indo-Pacific. *Asia Studies Centre, Research Paper no. 2/2018.* London : Henry Jackson Society, 2018.

Harris, Peter. 2020. A Rules-Based Order for the Indo-Pacific? *Journal of Indo-Pacific Affairs.* 2020.

US Department of State. 2019. A Free and Open Indo-Pacific: Advancing a Shared Vision. *Department of State, US Government.* [Online] 2019. https://www.state.gov/wp-content/uploads/2019/11/Free-and-Open-Indo-Pacific-4Nov2019.pdf .

—. 2020. Briefing with Senior State Department Officials on Secretary Pompeo's Visit to Japan. *US Department of State.* [Online] 2020. https://2017-2021.state.gov/briefing-with-senior-state-department-officials-on-secretary-pompeos-visit-to-japan/index.html.

Australian Government. 2017. Australia in the Asian Country. *Australian Government.* [Online] 2017. https://www.defence.gov.au/whitepaper/2013/docs/australia_in_the_asian_century_white_paper.pdf.

Scott, David. 2018. The Indo-Pacific in US Strategy: Responding to Power Shifts. *Rising Powers Quarterly.* 2018, Vol. 3, 2.

US Mission to ASEAN. 2017. Remarks by President Trump at APEC CEO Summit, Da Nang, Vietnam. *US Mission to ASEAN.* [Online] 2017. https://asean.usmission.gov/remarks-president-trump-apec-ceo-summit-da-nang-vietnam/.

Basu, Pratnashree, Saha, Roshan and Bhowmick, Soumya. 2021. *Connecting Distant Geographies: The EU in the Indo-Pacific.* [ORF Occasional Paper No. 329] s.l. : Observer Research Foundation, 2021.

Morcos, Pierre. 2021. The European Union Is Shaping Its Strategy for the Indo-Pacific. *Center for Strategic and International Studies.* [Online] 2021. https://www.csis.org/analysis/european-union-shaping-its-strategy-indo-pacific.

European Commission. 2018. Connecting Europe and Asia - Building blocks for an EU Strategy. *EEAS.* [Online] 2018. https://eeas.europa.eu/sites/default/files/joint_communication_-_connecting_europe_and_asia_-_building_blocks_for_an_eu_strategy_2018-09-19.pdf.

Nye, Joseph S. 2019. The rise and fall of American hegemony from Wilson to Trump. *International Affairs.* 2019, Vol. 95, 1.

—. **2018.** Donald Trump and the Decline of US Soft Power. *Project Syndicate.* [Online] 2018. https://www.project-syndicate.org/commentary/trump-american-soft-power-decline-by-joseph-s--nye-2018-02.

Smith, Tony. 2017. *Why Wilson matters: the origin of American liberal internationalism and its crisis today.* Princeton : Princeton University Press, 2017.

Pulipaka, Sanjay and Musaddi, Mohit. 2021. In Defence of the Indo-Pacific Concept. *ORF Issue Brief No. 493.* s.l. : Observer Research Foundation, 2021.

Koga, Kei. 2020. Japan's 'Indo-Pacific' Question: Countering China or Shaping a New Regional Order? *International Affairs.* 2020, Vol. 96, 1.

—. **2020.** Next Priorities for Japan's FOIP Vision: The Quad, ASEAN, and Institutional Linkages in the Indo-Pacific. *Journal of Indo-Pacific Affairs.* 2020.

Ministry of Foreign Affairs of Japan. 2018. Japan- Australia- India- U.S. Consultations. *Ministry of Foreign Affairs of Japan.* [Online] 2018. https://www.mofa.go.jp/press/release/press4e_002062.html .

Basu, Titli. 2020. India's Indo-Pacific Reckoning. *Journal of Indo-Pacific Affairs.* 2020.

Krishnan, Ananth. 2020. For minor tactical gains on the ground, China has strategically lost India, says former Indian Ambassador to China . *The Hindu.* [Online] 2020.

United Nations Statistics Division. 2000. National Accounts Main Aggregates Database. *United Nations Statistics Division, Economics and Statistics Branch.* [Online] 2000.

Bachhawat, Aakriti, et al. 2020. Critical technologies and the Indo-Pacific: A new India–Australia partnership. *ASPI, ORF Policy Brief 39/2020.* s.l. : Observer Research Foundation, 2020.

Sharma, Mihir, Kasliwal, Ria and Mukhopadhyay, Abhijit. 2021. Resilient, Inclusive, and Free: Towards a Post-Pandemic Indo-Pacific Region. *Observer Research Foundation.* 2021.

Sharma, Mihir and Bhogal, Preety. 2017. India and Global Trade Governance: Redefining Its 'National' Interest. *Observer Research Foundation.* 2017.

Bajpai, Prableen. 2021. Why China Is "The World's Factory". *Investopedia.* [Online] 2021. https://www.investopedia.com/articles/investing/102214/why -china-worlds-factory.asp.

Garton, Phil and Chang, Jennifer. 2005. The Chinese currency: how undervalued and how much does it matter? [online]. 2005. *Australian Government.* [Online] 2005.

Tan, Huileng. 2018. China is letting the yuan crush the dollar — Trump is just one reason why. *CNBC.* [Online] 2018. https://www.cnbc.com/2018/02/22/chinese-yuan-against-the-dollar-china-currency-appreciation.html.

Kumar, K. Bharat. 2020. Why has Japan mooted the Supply Chain Resilience Initiative? *The Hindu.* [Online] 2020.

https://www.thehindu.com/business/Economy/what-is-the-new-idea-on-supply-chains/article32476160.ece.

Press Information Bureau, Government of India. 2021. India and Australia must work towards enhancing the resilience of supply chains and greater engagement in the Indo-Pacific region. *Press Information Bureau, Government of India.* [Online] 2021. https://pib.gov.in/PressReleseDetailm.aspx?PRID=1758616 .

Burton, Melanie. 2020. Australian, India, sign joint deal on critical minerals. *Reuters.* [Online] 2020. https://www.reuters.com/article/india-australia-critical-minerals/australian-india-sign-joint-deal-on-critical-minerals-idUSL4N2DH287.

Ministry of External Affairs, Government of India. 2020. India at UNSC 2021-22. *Ministry of External Affairs, Government of India.* [Online] 2020. https://www.mea.gov.in/Images/amb1/INDIAUNSC.pdf.

Agarwal, Man Mohan. 1983. INDIA AND THE UNCTAD. *India Quarterly.* 1983, Vol. 39, 4.

Sridharan, Srinath. 2022. Governance push for corporate India. *Observer Research Foundation.* [Online] 8 January 2022. https://www.orfonline.org/expert-speak/governance-push-for-corporate-india/.

Jha, Ramanath. 2022. Transparency as a tool for urban local governance. *Observer Research Foundation.* [Online] 8 January 2022. https://www.orfonline.org/expert-speak/transparency-as-a-tool-for-urban-local-governance/.

Shaw, Kiran Mazumdar. 2020. The challenges and opportunities of innovating in India . *Observer Research Foundation.* [Online] 30 October 2020. https://www.orfonline.org/expert-speak/challenges-opportunities-innovating-india/.

Chaudhary, Dipanjan Roy. 2018. Europe, Japan, US, UAE prefer India for joint infrastructure projects in Africa. *Economic Times.* [Online] 24 November 2018. https://economictimes.indiatimes.com/news/economy/infrastructure/europe-japan-us-uae-prefer-india-for-joint-infrastructure-projects-in-africa/articleshow/66780251.cms?from=mdr.

Sinha, Manish. 2017. India on the Worlds Infrastructure Map. *dun & bradstreet.* [Online] 10 November 2017.

https://www.dnb.co.in/perspective/thought-leadership/india-in-worlds-infrastructure-map.

Jaishankar, Dhruva. 2021. Exploring India's economic diplomacy with the US. *Observer Research Foundation.* [Online] 26 April 2021. https://www.orfonline.org/expert-speak/exploring-india-economic-diplomacy-us/.

Aurobindo, Sri. 1997. *The Rennaisance in India and Other Essays on Indian Culture.* s.l. : Sri Aurobindo Ashram Trust, 1997.

Strategic Studies Quarterly. 2018. Conventional Deterrence: An Interview with John J. Mearsheimer. *Strategic Studies Quarterly.* 2018, Vol. 12, 4.

Walt, Stephen M. 2018. US grand strategy after the Cold War: Can realism explain it? Should realism guide it? *International Relations.* 2018, Vol. 32, 1.

Onuf, Nicholas. 2013. *World of Our Making: Rules and Rule in Social Theory and International Relations.* New York : Routledge, 2013.

Wetering, Carina van de. 2018. Mistrust amongst democracies: Constructing US-India insecurity during the Cold War. [book auth.] Hiski Haukkala and Carina van de Wetering. [ed.] J. Vuorelma. *Trust in international relations: Rationalist, constructivist and psychological approaches.* s.l. : Routledge, 2018.

Mignolo, Walter D. 2017. Coloniality Is Far from Over, and So Must Be Decoloniality. *Afterall.* 2017, Vol. 43.

Trouillt, Michael-Rolph. 2002. North Atlantic Universals: Analytical Fictions, 1492-1945. *The South Atlantic Quarterly.* 2002, Vol. 100, 4.

Chatterjee, Partha. 1993. *Nationalist Thought and the Colonial World: A Derivative Discourse.* Minneapolis : University of Minnesota Press, 1993.

Ikenberry, G. John. 2010. The Liberal International Order and its Discontents. *Millenium.* 2010, Vol. 38, 3.

Bauman, Zygmunt. 2011. Intervista sull'identità . [ed.] B. Vecchi. *Laterza.* 2011.

Hobsbawm, Eric and Ranger, Terence. 1983. *The Invention of Tradition.* s.l. : Cambridge University Press, 1983.

Hofferberth, Matthias and Weber, Christian. 2015. Lost in Translation: A Critique of Constructivist Norm Research. *Journal of International Relations and Development.* 2015, Vol. 18, 1.

Anant, T. C. A. 2001. India and the WTO: Flawed Rejectionist Approach. *Economic and Political Weekly.* 2001, Vol. 36, 45.

Dabhade, Manish. 2017. India's Pursuit of United Nations Security Council Reforms. *Observer Research Foundation.* [Online] 2017.

Narlikar, A. 2007. All that Glitters is Not Gold: India's Rise to Power. *Third World Quarterly.* 2007, Vol. 28, 5.

Kanth, D. 2016. What Happened at Nairobi and Why. *Economic and Political Weekly Insight.* 2016, Vol. 2, 11.

Chanda, R. and Gopalan, S. 2007. GATS and Developments in India's Service Sector. [ed.] Suparna Karmakar, Rajiv Kumar and Bibek Debroy. *India's Liberalisation Experience: Hostage to the WTO?* s.l. : SAGE Publications India Pvt. Ltd, 2007.

Anholt, Simon. 2020. *The Good Country Equation: How We Can Repair the World in One Generation.* s.l. : Berrett-Koehler Publishers, 2020.

Bommakanti, Kartik. 2017. India's Evolving Views on Responsibility to Protect (R2P) and Humanitarian Interventions: The Significance of Legitimacy. *Observer Research Foundation.* [Online] 2017.

Claude, I. L. 1996. Collective Legitimation as a Political Function of the UN. *International Organization.* 1996, Vol. 20, 3.

Office of the Spokesperson. 2022. Joint Statement on Quad Cooperation in the Indo-Pacific. *US Department of State.* [Online] 11 February 2022. https://www.state.gov/joint-statement-on-quad-cooperation-in-the-indo-pacific/.

Chaudhary, Dipanjan Roy. 2022. India takes different line on Myanmar, Ukraine. *Economic Times.* [Online] 12 February 2022. https://economictimes.indiatimes.com/news/india/india-takes-different-line-on-myanmar-ukraine/articleshow/89516125.cms?utm_source=contentofinterest&utm_medium=text&utm_campaign=cppst.

Vennet, Nikolas Vander and Salman, Mohammad. 2019. Strategic Hedging and Changes in Geopolitical Capabilities for Second-Tier States. *Chinese Political Science Review.* 2019, Vol. 4.

Kumar, Mohan. 2019. India's embrace of strategic hedging. *Hindustan Times.* [Online] 9 September 2019. https://epaper.hindustantimes.com/Home/ShareArticle?OrgId=2cdd5644.

EEAS. 2021a. EU Strategy for Cooperation in the Indo-Pacific. *EEAS.* [Online] 2021a.

https://eeas.europa.eu/headquarters/headquarters-homepage/96741/eu-strategy-cooperation-indo-pacific_en.

—. **2021b.** The EU needs a strategic approach for the Indo-Pacific. [Online] 2021b. https://eeas.europa.eu/headquarters/headquarters-homepage/94898/eu-needs-strategic-approach-indo-pacific_en.

Ministry of External Affairs, Government of India. 2021b. Statement by Foreign Secretary at UNSC high-level meeting on "Maintenance of international peace and security: upholding multilateralism and the United Nations-centered international system". *Ministry of External Affairs, Government of India.* [Online] 2021b. https://www.mea.gov.in/Speeches-Statements.htm?dtl/33851/Statement+by+Foreign+Secretary+at+UNSC+highlevel+meeting+on+Maintenance+of+international+peace+and+security+upholding+multilateralism+and+the+United+Nationscentered+international+system.

—. **2021a.** Joint Statement on Inaugural India-Australia 2+2 Ministerial Dialogue (11 September 2021, New Delhi). *Ministry of External Affairs, Government of India.* [Online] 2021a.

Abhivardhan and Sekhar, Bhavana J. 2021a. *Global Customary International Law Index: An Analytical Monograph.* Allahabad : AbhiGlobal Legal Research & Media LLP,, 2021a.

Abhivardhan, et al. 2021b. [ed.] Abhivardhan. *Regulatory Sovereignty in India: Indigenizing Competition-Technology Approaches, ISAIL-TR-001.* s.l. : Indian Society of Artificial Intelligence and Law Charitable Trust, 2021b.

Chikermane, Gautam and Agarwal, Rishi. 2022. *Jailed for Doing Business: The 26,134 Imprisonment Clauses in India's Business Laws.* s.l. : Observer Research Foundation, 2022.

Internationalism Global Podcasts. 2022. #GLACon2022 | Panel 1 | India as a Neutral Hub of ADRs. *YouTube.* [Online] 2022. https://www.youtube.com/watch?v=dGcNMytHI-w.

List of Figures